HELLO

MY NAME IS:

My birthday

My signature

My AWESOME Year Being 7

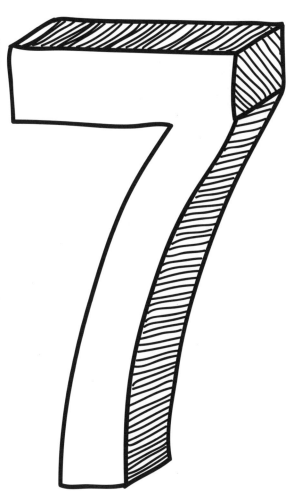

Published by Collins
An imprint of HarperCollins Publishers
Westerhill Road
Bishopbriggs
Glasgow G64 2QT

First edition 2020

10 9 8 7 6 5 4 3 2 1

ISBN 978-0-00-837261-3

A catalogue record for this book is available from the British Library

ACKNOWLEDGEMENTS
Publisher: Michelle l'Anson
Concept creator: Fiona McGlade
Author and Illustrator: Kia Marie Hunt
Project Manager: Robin Scrimgeour
Designer: Kevin Robbins
Photos © Shutterstock

Special thanks to the children at Golcar Junior Infant and Nursery School

Printed by GPS Group, Slovenia

MIX
Paper from responsible sources
FSC www.fsc.org
FSC™ C007454

This book is produced from independently certified FSC™ paper to ensure responsible forest management.

For more information visit: www.harpercollins.co.uk/green

My AWESOME Year Being

Written and illustrated by
Kia Marie Hunt

Contents

6 Hello!
7 Rules
8 All about me
10 A day in my life
12 My amazing family
14 6 things I liked about being 6
15 8 things I want to do before I am 8
16 My favourite song
17 Sharing songs
18 Life outside
20 Mountain hike!
22 Recipe: Ice lollies & yoghurt pops
26 I ♡ school
28 My fantastic friends
30 The supermarket search challenge
32 Scavenger hunt
36 My favourite book
37 Being a 7-year-old bookworm
38 My travels around the world
40 Make a mosaic
42 My holiday
44 Sports superstar
46 My favourite sport
48 Water party!
52 My favourite food
54 Writing a short story
58 Making a bird feeder
60 Planning the ultimate sleepover

62 Recipe: Remarkable rainbow cupcakes
64 My favourite film
65 Sharing films
66 Visiting a farmers' market
68 Keep on moving!
69 We're going on a bug hunt...
72 Being a 7-year-old teacher
74 Playing crazy golf
76 What makes me excited
78 Visiting a botanical garden
80 Being a 7-year-old astronaut
82 My favourite game
83 Sharing games
84 Making a kite
88 Trying yoga
92 Furry friends
94 Learning a new language
96 Recipe: Spooky eyeball pasta
98 Wacky races
100 Pavement chalks
102 Creating a new character
104 Family are friends too!
106 Inventing a new sport
108 What makes me laugh
110 Quizzing my friends
112 Welcome to the talent show!
114 Designing my dream home
116 Visiting a planetarium
118 My favourite outfit
119 Being a 7-year-old fashion designer

Hello!

Your year being 7 is going to be **AWESOME** now that you have this book to record it in!

You're about to discover **SO MANY** fun activities, projects, recipes, and other exciting new things to try...

Start by writing your name, birthday and signature at the front of the book.

Near the end of the book, there are blank pages where you can continue with any of the activities, try something again, or just do whatever you like!

Just inside the back cover, you can draw or write about a fun thing you did for each month of your awesome year being 7!

P.S. You might need a grown-up's help to do some of the things in this book, so ask them to read the note on page 128.

~~Rules~~

1. Do the activities in this book in any order you like.
2. You could use pencils, pens, highlighters, crayons or paints to answer the questions. Feel free to make a mess!
3. Why not colour in the drawings?
4. Why not add your own doodles?

5. You can write your answers, draw, or even stick photos in. Do it your own way!
6. HAVE FUN and remember that you are awesome!

All about **me**

What do you look like?

(Draw yourself.)

Where do you live?

What are you good at?

What is awesome about you?

Who gave you this book?

(Remember to say thank you to them.
They are fantastic!)

A **day** in my life

This page is all about your day!

What are the first 3 things you do when you wake up each morning?

1. ....
2. ....
3. ....

What is your favourite part of the day and why?

....

....

....

....

What do you like to eat for...

Breakfast?

Lunch?

Your evening meal?

Draw or write in the shapes.

What are the last 3 things you do before going to sleep?

1 ....

2 ....

3 ....

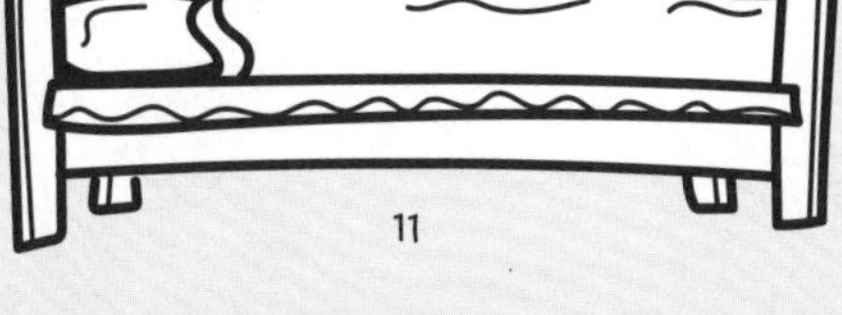

My amazing **family**

How many people are in your family?...........

List their names:

....

....

Draw your family here:

Don't forget to include yourself!

What is the best thing about your family?

What is the best thing your family do together?

6 things I liked about being 6

What were the 6 best things about being a 6-year-old? Write or draw them inside each shape.

8 things I want to do before I am **8**

You don't have to do this all in one go. You can add some things then come back to it later.

Think of 8 things you want to do before you are 8. Perhaps you'd like to try something you've never done before, or want to visit somewhere new?

Write them down and tick each one off when you've done it.

1. .... ☐
2. .... ☐
3. .... ☐
4. .... ☐
5. .... ☐
6. .... ☐
7. .... ☐
8. .... ☐

My favourite **song**

What is the name of your favourite song?

Who sings it?

What's your favourite line in the song?

How does this song make you feel?

Sharing **songs**

Ask a friend or someone in your family what their favourite song is and then listen to it together.

Who did you ask?

What was their favourite song?

Who sings it?

Did you like it?

Life **outside**

Do you often spend time outside?

When you play outside, where do you go?

Who do you spend time outside with?

What is your favourite activity to do outside?

When it's sunny outside I like to...

When it's raining outside I like to....

When it's snowing outside I like to...

Mountain **hike!**

Grab your walking boots, some snacks for energy, and a bottle of water – it's hiking time! You can make your hike as easy or as difficult as you like, whether that's walking up a small hill or trekking up a big mountain.

Date: ______________________________

BE SAFE! Always go hiking with a grown-up.

Where did you go on your hike?

____

What did it look like?

Draw it or stick in a photo.

TIP Why not play 'I spy' on your hike?

Who did you go with? ______________________________

____

As you go along, draw or write down a list of anything interesting you see on your hike!

(This could include plants, animals, birds, other people, or anything else you like!)

Recipe: Ice lollies & yoghurt pops

How to make

There are loads of different ways to make ice lollies and yoghurt pops, so you're in for a treat! Choose your own way:

1. Pick your choice of **container**, **stick**, and **flavour**.
2. Add the ingredients for your chosen flavour into the containers, and put the sticks in the middle.
3. Pop them in the freezer overnight, simple!

Containers

You could use all sorts of containers to freeze your ice lollies or yoghurt pops into many weird and wonderful shapes. Here are some ideas:

- A normal ice lolly tray (or ice lolly moulds)
- Cups (any shape or size)
- Cupcake cases (best for less runny flavours)
- An ice cube tray (for minis!)
- Empty yoghurt pots

Sticks

If you have some ice lolly sticks in the house, great! If not, you could use any of these instead:

- Spoons
- Straws
- Chopsticks!

These frozen treats are so good you'll want to eat them whatever the weather!

Mmm!

Flavours

Now for the most exciting part! Choose one of the flavour recipes below or experiment with other ingredients you may already have in the house…

Watermelon ice lollies

- Ask a grown-up to help you prepare some juicy watermelon chunks with the seeds taken out.
- Whizz them all up in a blender with a bit of lemon juice and a lot of honey.

Berrylicious yoghurt pops

- Mush up a few handfuls of strawberries, raspberries and blueberries.
- Mix them with some vanilla (or strawberry) yoghurt.

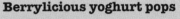

Banana and honey yoghurt pops

- Mush up one ripe banana.
- Mix it with some Greek or plain yoghurt and a big spoonful of honey (and some granola if you like).

Creamy coconut ice lollies

- Ask a grown-up to cut open a ripe avocado.
- Take out the big stone and scoop the creamy avocado out of the skin.
- With a grown-up's help, put the avocado into a blender with some coconut milk and coconut flakes, then whizz it all up!
- Add some sugar or honey to make it sweeter.

Date: ....

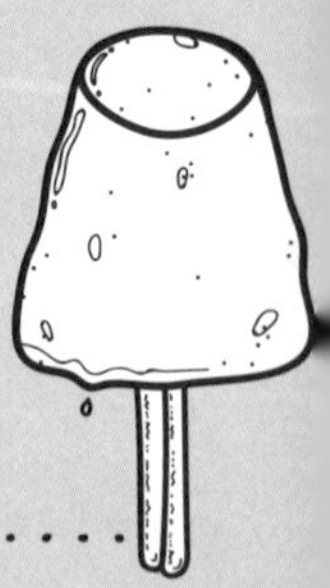

Where did you make your ice lollies or yoghurt pops?

....

Who did you make them with?

....

What containers did you use?

....

What did you use for your sticks?

....

What flavour ice lollies or yoghurt pops did you make?

....

What did they look like?

Draw them or stick in a photo.

Rate this recipe out of 5

1=Yuck!
5=Yum!

What did they taste like?

What was the best thing about making this recipe?

....

....

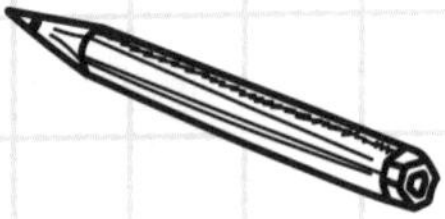

I ♡ school

What is your school called?

What year are you in?

Who is your teacher?

What is your favourite subject? Why?

What is your least-favourite subject?

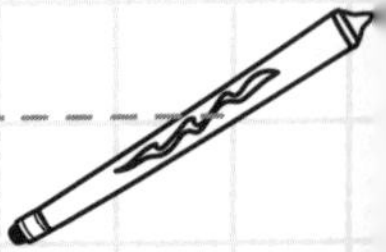

What is the best thing about going to school?

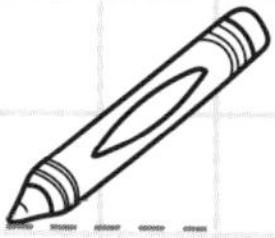

If you were suddenly in charge of the school, what changes would you make?

My fantastic **friends**

Who are your friends?

List their names and write down what you like about them.

Name of friend	What I like about them

What do you like to do with your friends?

Who is your best friend and why?

Draw your best friend or stick a photo here:

What is your favourite memory with your best friend?

You can write or draw.

The **supermarket** search challenge

Going to the supermarket doesn't have to be boring! Try out these fun challenges:

Task 1: Create a colourful shopping list

Most grown-ups need a shopping list when they go to the supermarket. Instead of letting them write it, ask them what they need, then you make the list! You can decorate it and make it as colourful as you like.

Task 2: Speedy shopping assistant

When you're at the supermarket, you will become the shopping assistant. Time how long it takes to find the items you need in each aisle, and see if you can beat your score – without running!

Task 3: Super silly search

While you're shopping, see if you can also spot these 4 silly items:

- Something with a funny face on the packet
- The most colourful thing you can find
- Something written in a different language
- A frozen food that looks disgusting!

Date: ....

Which supermarket did you go to and who did you go with?

....

....

Rate how much you enjoyed each of the tasks:

Task 1: 

Task 2: 

Task 3: 

What was the best thing about doing the supermarket search challenge?

....

Next time make up 4 'Super silly search' items of your own and add them to the shopping list!

Scavenger **hunt**

Draw them or stick in photos.

Take a walk outside and go on a scavenger hunt. See how many of these things you can find...

Date: ______________________

1. Find something that smells very nice. ☐
   What is it, and what does it look like?

2. Find something that smells horrible. ☐
   What is it, and what does it look like?

REMEMBER! You don't have to find these things in order!

3 Find something that has an interesting texture. ☐

What is it, and what does it look like?

4 Find something that starts with the first letter of your name. ☐

What is it, and what does it look like?

5 Find something smaller than your little finger. ☐

What is it, and what does it look like?

6 Find something that's much bigger than you! ☐

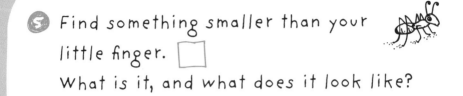

What is it, and what does it look like?

7 Find something that's really old. ☐
What is it, and what does it look like?

8 Find something that you think could be a treasure. ☐
What is it, and what does it look like?

If you ticked off all 8 items, well done!

You just completed your scavenger hunt.

My favourite **book**

What is your favourite book?

Who is your favourite character?

Draw or write about them.

What is your favourite part of the story?

Draw or write about it.

Being a 7-year-old **bookworm**

Every time you read a book that you like, write the title below.

My **travels** around the **world**

What country do you live in?

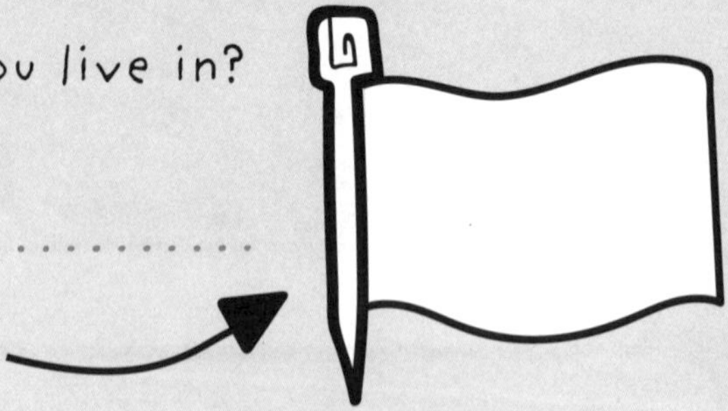

Draw its flag here:

Have you visited any other countries?

If you have, name them and draw their flags below. If you haven't, make up some new countries and draw some new flags!

Which other countries would you like to visit?

Name them and draw their flags here. Next to each one, write why you would like to visit.

Make a mosaic

The Romans loved to decorate with amazing mosaics made from loads of small tiles. Here's a fun and easy way to make your own.

What you'll need

- Coloured paper or magazines you can cut up
- A big white sheet of paper
- A pencil
- Scissors
- Glue
- Tubs (optional)

How to make

1. To make your coloured tiles, cut up your coloured paper (or pages from magazines) into small squares.
2. Sort your paper tiles into groups of each colour. You can put them in little piles or use tubs to keep them separate.
3. Draw your mosaic design onto your sheet of paper. Draw lightly with the pencil, and make sure your design has big shapes you can easily fill in with your tiles. Here are some design ideas:
   - Your favourite animal
   - A flower, plant or tree
   - The sun or the moon
4. Now, stick your tiles down using different colours for different areas. Bring your mosaic masterpiece to life!

You can also search online for printable mosaic patterns.

Date: ______________________

What design did you choose for your mosaic?

____

What does your finished mosaic look like?

Draw it or stick in a photo.

What was the best thing about making your mosaic?

____

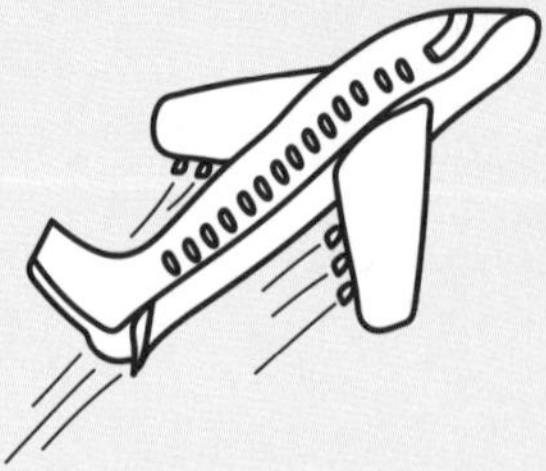

My **holiday**

Think of a holiday or special trip you have been on recently.

Where did you go?

When did you go?

How did you get there?

Who did you go with?

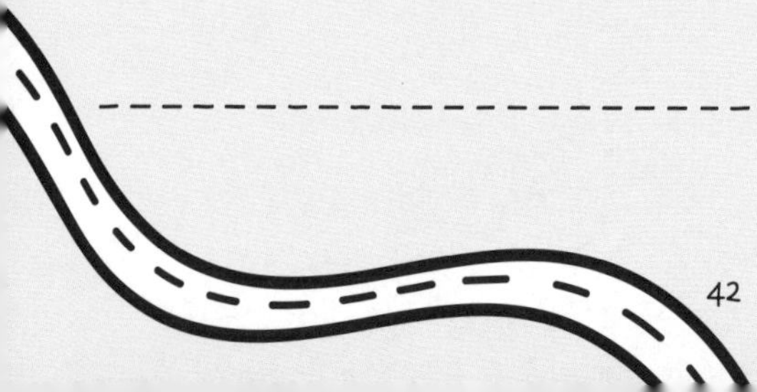

What was your favourite part of the holiday or trip? Why?

Do you have any photos from your holiday or trip? Stick one here.

(Or you could draw the place you visited instead.)

Sports superstar

What sports do you do?

Which sport are you best at?

Do you think being good at sport is important?

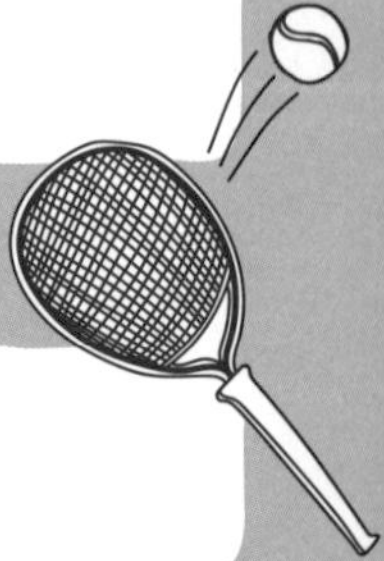

Why or why not?

How does playing sports make you feel?

Have you ever taken part in a sports competition, race, match or tournament?

Where was it?

When was it?

What did you like most about taking part in it? Why?

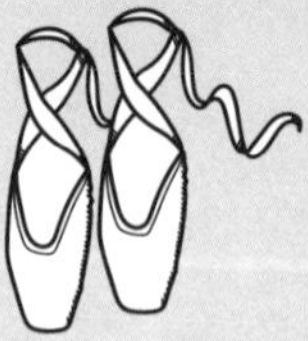

My favourite **sport**

What is your favourite sport?

Why is it your favourite?

Rate how well you think you can play your favourite sport:

1 = I'm rubbish – but I love it anyway!

2 = I'm still learning...

3 = I'm quite good

4 = I'm very good

5 = I'm an expert!

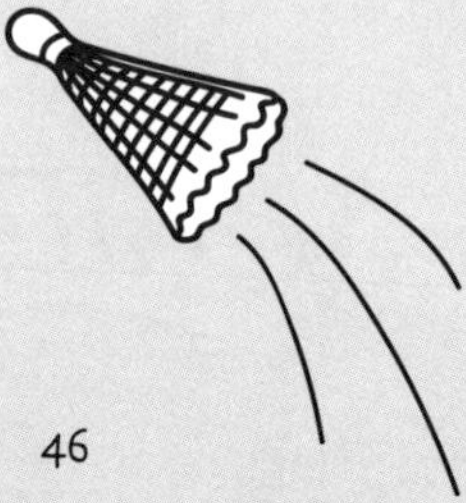

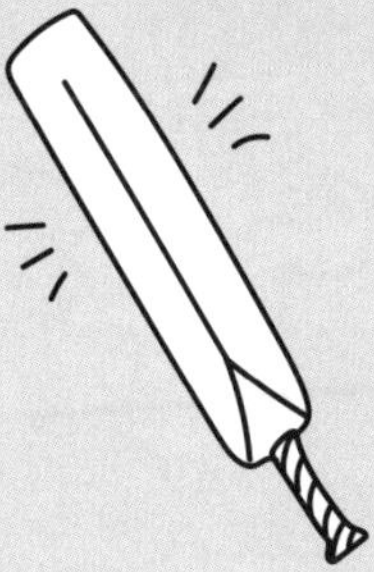

Where do you usually play your favourite sport?

Who do you usually play it with?

If you could be amazing at any sport, which one would it be?

Water party!

On a warm and sunny day, use some of these fun ideas to host your own water party!

Frozen races

- The night before your water party, put some small plastic toys into cups of water and leave them in the freezer overnight.
- The next day, take the toys out of the cups – they will now be surrounded by big blocks of ice.
- Make a ramp and race your frozen toys down it.

You can also play a game to see who can melt their frozen toy first!

Dizzy waiter

- Set up trays of reusable plastic cups, full of water.
- Split into 2 teams.
- Someone from each team has to spin around 5 times, pick up a tray and race to a bucket, trying not to spill the water!
- Pour in any water that's left in the cups – the first team to fill their bucket is the winner!

Waterslide slip

- All you need for this is a big plastic sheet or 'tarp', a hose, and something to make your slide slippery, like washing-up liquid.
- Ask a grown-up to help you set up your homemade slide, then take turns to slip and slide along it.
- See who can slide the furthest.

Water balloon games

For these games, you will need to fill up lots of water balloons before the party – or you could turn it into a race by seeing who can fill all of their balloons up the fastest!

Use biodegradable ones and pick up the bits afterwards!

Water balloon tennis

- Can you hit the water balloon to each other without it popping? Find out!
- You can use a tennis racket, or you can make your own water balloon bats by sticking a big sponge to the end of a long stick.

Water balloon toss

- Line up 5 colourful buckets or plastic bowls.
- Each person has 5 water balloons to toss into the buckets.
- Getting a balloon into the closest bucket is worth 5 points, then 10, 20, 30, and 40.
- You can make a sign or label for each bowl and make a points chart to help you add up who has won.

Splat!

Soaked!

Water balloon towel fling

- In pairs, hold a towel out with a water balloon sitting on the top of it.
- Both pull the towel tightly at the same time to toss the balloon up into the air and over to the other team.
- The other team have to catch it in their towel – if it explodes, the throwing team gets a point!

Splash!

Turn the page...

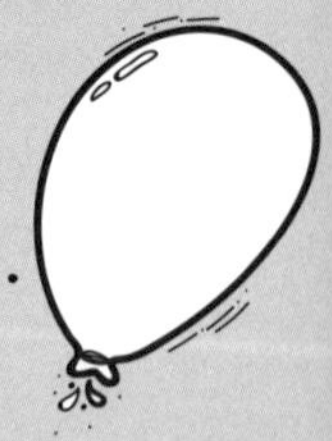

Date:

Where did you have your water party?

Who did you invite?

What water games did you play?

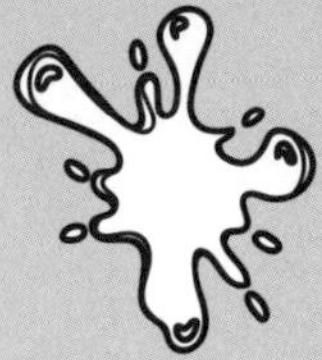

Which game was the most fun? Why?

Draw your favourite memory from the water party, or stick some photos here:

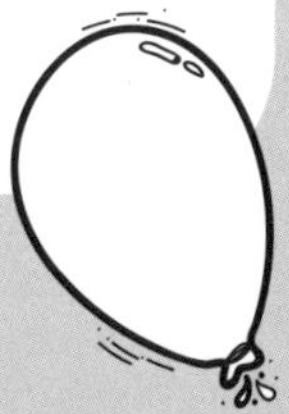

My favourite **food**

What is your favourite meal?

Draw it here!

How often do you eat it?

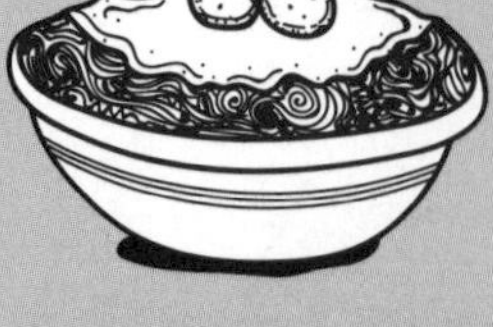

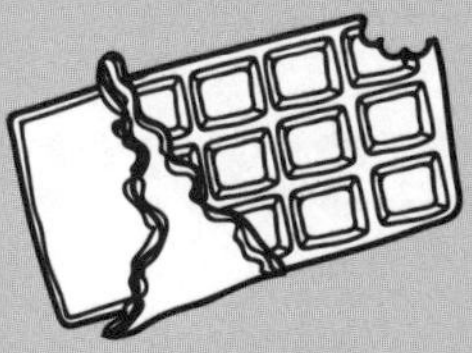

What is your favourite sweet food?

....

Draw it here!

How often do you eat it?

....

Writing a short **story**

Write a short story about anything you like.

It could be a funny story, a scary story, an adventure story, or a silly story! You could even base it on a book or character you already know, or write a sequel (a new part to that story).

Who will be the main character, and where will your story be set?

Draw your main character and story setting.

How will your short story start?

(How will you introduce and build up your character and setting?)

What will the main character have to overcome?

(This could be a mystery to solve, something to find,
a quest to complete, or an enemy to defeat!)

How will the short story end?

Start writing your story on this page.

(If it gets too long, you can carry on by using the blank pages at the back of the book, or any other paper you have!)

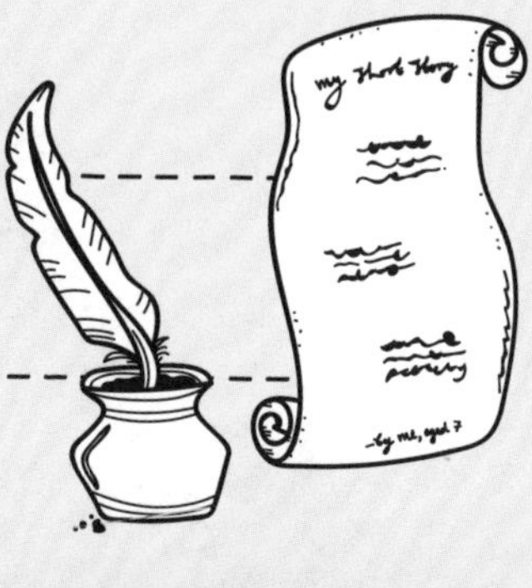
my Short Story
-by me, aged 7

Making a **bird feeder**

See how many birds you can attract with this tasty, tempting treat for them...

What you'll need

- A cardboard tube (why not recycle an empty toilet roll?)
- A plate
- Some wool or string
- Some bird seed
- Peanut butter
- A spoon

How to make

1. Use the spoon to scoop peanut butter out of the jar and spread it all over the cardboard tube. Messy but fun!
2. Pour some bird seed onto the plate and roll your peanut butter tube through the seeds until it is completely covered.
3. Then put your piece of string or wool through the middle of the tube, lift up the bird feeder by both ends, and carry it to where you want it to hang.
4. Ask a grown-up to help you tie it in place on a tree branch or somewhere else that's quite high up. (Far away from pesky cats!)

Now, simply sit back and watch... The only thing more fun than making your own bird feeder is watching all the birds that come to visit once you hang it up!

TIP! Do this on a dry day, or hang it somewhere sheltered so it doesn't get soggy!

Date:

Where did you hang your bird feeder?

Draw it or stick in a photo.

Which birds came to eat from your bird feeder?

Use the bird identifier on the RSPB website (www.rspb.org.uk).

Name them, and draw or stick in photos.

Planning the ultimate **sleepover**

Everyone loves a great sleepover! Plan your ultimate sleepover or pyjama party here...

Where will it be?

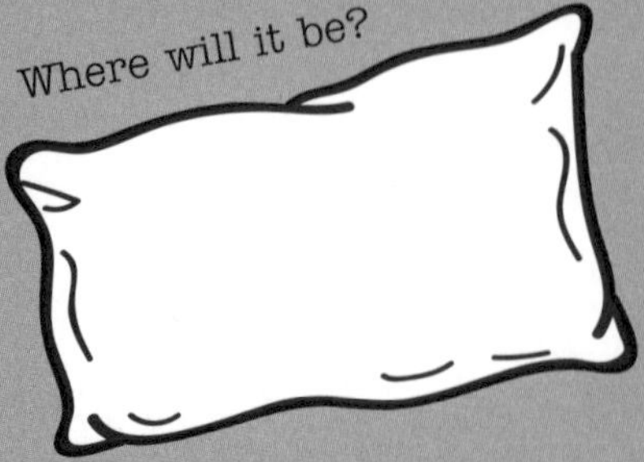

When will it be?

Who will be invited?

What ultimate sleepover snacks will you eat?

Ideas: Popcorn, trail mix, fruit – or you could make rainbow cupcakes **on the next page!**

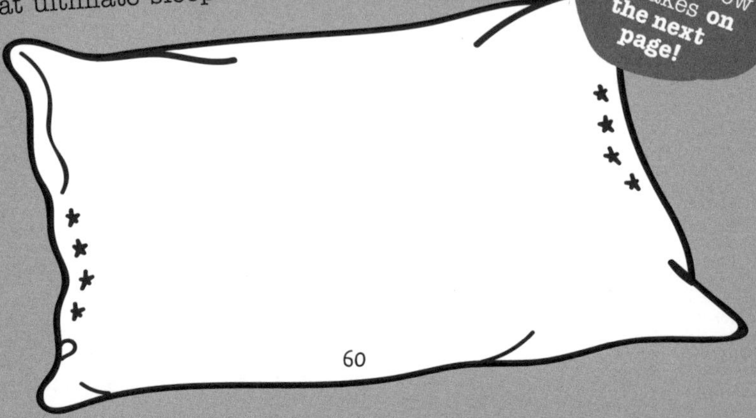

What ultimate sleepover activities will you do?

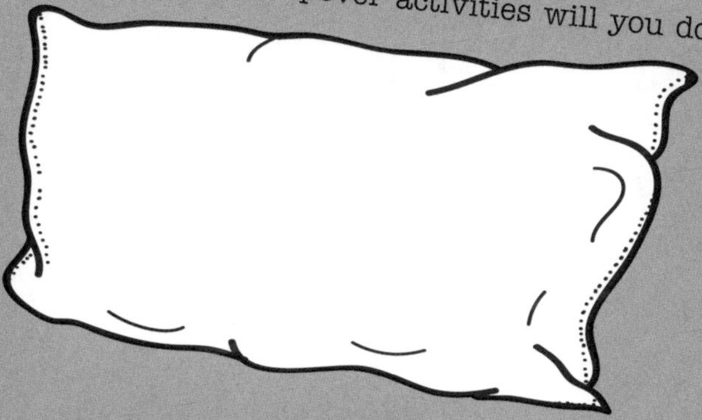

Ideas:
Watch a film, tell spooky stories, play games, make crafts, or maybe even do something from this book together...

Rate your ultimate sleepover experience:

What was your favourite part (or funniest moment) of the sleepover?

Write, draw, or stick in a photo.

What time did you go to sleep?

Recipe: Remarkable rainbow **cupcakes**

What you'll need

- Packet cake mix (500g usually makes about 16 cakes)
- A muffin tray and some cupcake cases
- White icing and rainbow sprinkles
- 1 big bowl and 7 small bowls
- Food colouring (blue, green, red and yellow)

TIP! Check the cake mix packet to see if you need any extra ingredients.

How to make

1. Ask a grown-up to preheat the oven.
2. In the big bowl, follow the instructions on the packet cake mix.
3. Once you have your cake mix, divide it equally into the 7 smaller bowls.
4. Now it's time to make your colours, by mixing different food colourings:

5. Put your cupcake cases into the muffin tray spaces.

6. In every cupcake case, add 7 layers of cake mix. You can add them in rainbow order or you can change the order if you like. (Just make sure to smooth each layer with a clean spoon before you add another layer on top!)
7. Ask a grown-up to help you bake the cakes by following the cake mix instructions.
8. When they are baked and cooled, cover them in white icing and rainbow sprinkles.

Date: ______________________________

How did your cupcakes taste?

Rate this recipe out of 5

1=Yuck!
5=Yum!

My favourite **film**

What is your favourite film?

____

How many times have you watched this film?

____

What is your favourite part of the film?

____

____

____

How does watching this film make you feel?

Sharing films

Ask a friend or someone in your family what their favourite film is and watch it together.

Who did you ask?

What was their favourite film?

Did you like it? Yes ☐ No ☐

Why or why not?

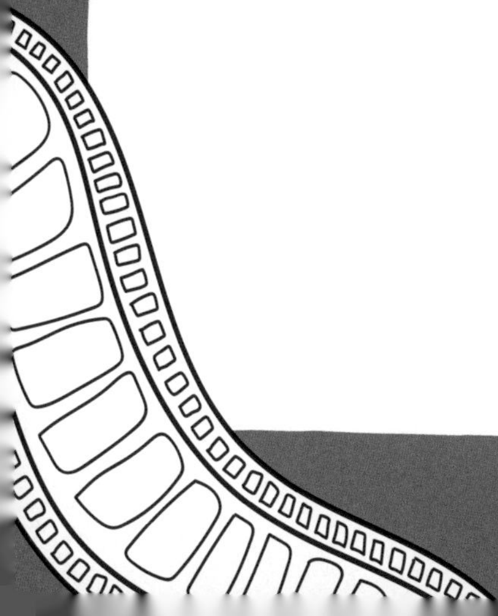

Visiting a **farmers' market**

Farmers' markets are full of amazing sights, with lots of colourful food and fresh produce to discover. Ask a grown-up to take you to one and describe your experience here...

Date: ____________________

Where was the farmers' market you visited?

____

____

Who did you go with?

____

There are usually some food and drink samples at farmers' markets. Try some out!

(Write down or draw what you tried.)

Being a 7-year-old taste tester!

Draw some things you liked from the farmers' market, or stick in photos.

(This could be a stall or food you liked, an interesting fruit or funny vegetable, an animal you saw, or anything else!)

Keep on **moving!**

What is your favourite exercise?

Where and when do you like to do your favourite exercise?

Are you good at it?

How does exercising make you feel?

We're going on a **bug hunt...**

Get your magnifying glass ready and go outside, you're going on a **big** hunt for **little** beasts!

Date:

Where will you be hunting for bugs?

Who will you be hunting with?

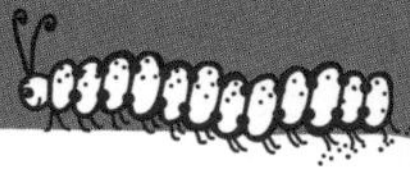

Fill in the **bug tracker** on the next page.

What was your favourite thing about hunting for bugs?

Rate this activity:

What bug is it? (This could be the name you call it, or the scientific name for the species.)	**Where did you see it?** (Was it under a rock? In the grass? In the air? On water? Somewhere else?)

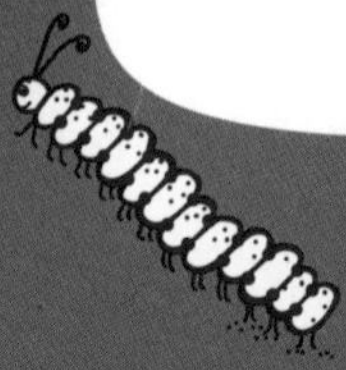

What does it look like? (Draw or describe it.)	**How many did you see?** (One? Three? Too many to count?!)

Being a 7-year-old **teacher**

If you could be the teacher of your class for one day, what subject lessons or classroom activities would you plan?

Breaktime

Lunchtime

As the teacher for the day, you get to invent 5 new school rules. What would they be?

My rules

1.

2.

3.

4.

5.

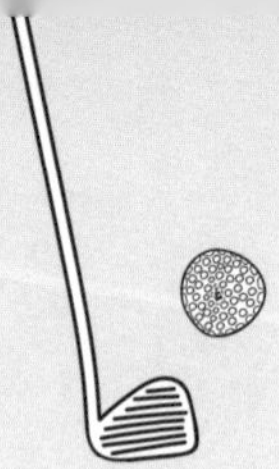

Playing **crazy golf**

Why did the golfer need a new pair of socks?

Because they got a hole-in-one!

Go to a crazy golf course with your friends or family and describe your experience here...

Date:

Where did you play crazy golf?

Who won?

Rate this activity:

You could also visit a mini golf or pitch and putt course.

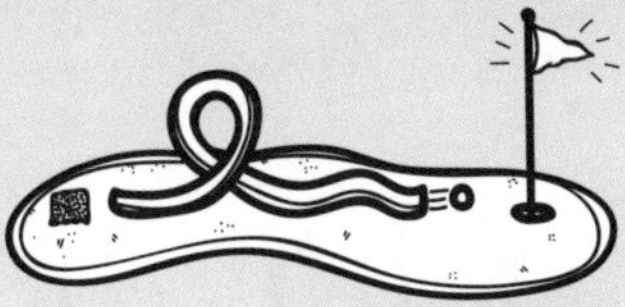

What was the best thing about your game of crazy golf?

Write, draw, or stick in a photo.

Design your own crazy golf hole here:

It can be as wacky as you like!

What makes me **excited**

What makes you feel excited?

(Write about, draw, or stick in photos of any activities, toys, songs, animals, people or places that are exciting to you.)

You don't have to do this all in one go. You can come back to it when something else exciting happens!

What is the most exciting thing that's ever happened to you?

What does being excited feel like? Can you describe it?

(If it's hard to describe it with words, draw how it feels, or draw what you look like when you get excited!)

Visiting a **botanical garden**

You can visit a tropical climate and discover weird and wonderful plants without ever leaving the country. Simply take a trip to a botanical garden, or a park with a tropical greenhouse!

Date: ___________________________________

Botanical garden or greenhouse visited:

____

Describe your visit in 3 words.

(How did the air feel? What could you see, smell or hear?)

____

____

____

Draw any interesting or strange-looking plants you saw, find out their names, and label them.

What was your favourite thing about visiting the gardens or greenhouse?

Would you visit again?

Being a 7-year-old **astronaut**

Imagine this: you've been travelling on your spaceship for years and years. You've just discovered a new planet in a solar system that no one else knew about...

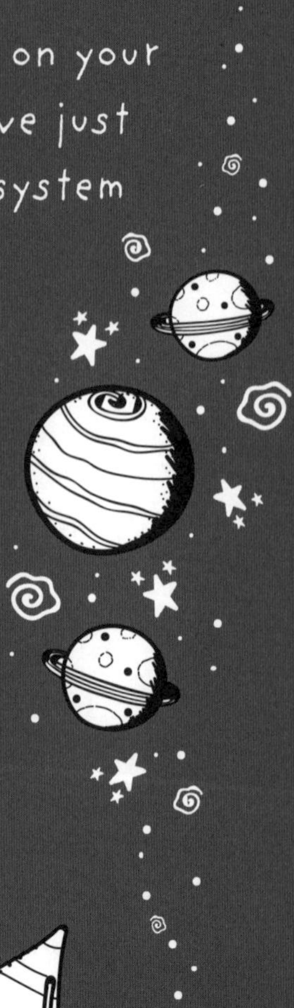

What would you call your newly discovered planet?

Draw what you think the new planet would look like:

How would it feel when you landed there?

The ground is:

(Rocky? Squishy? Fluffy? Slimy? Something else?)

The sky is:

(Dark and stormy? Full of rainbows? Something else?)

The weather is:

(Hot and sticky? Freezing? Raining gemstones? Something else?)

If you discovered a new creature that lives on the planet, what would it look like?

Write its name too!

My favourite **game**

What is your favourite game?

What is the game about?

Where do you like to play it?

Who do you like to play it with?

Sharing games

Ask a friend or someone in your family what their favourite game is and play it together.

Who did you ask?

What was their favourite game?

Did you like it? Why or why not?

Making a **kite**

Let's go fly a kite! (But we need to make it first!)

What you will need

- An A4 piece of paper or thin card
- String (any type, but kite string is best)
- Wooden skewers (or skinny bamboo sticks, or straws)
- Ribbon of any colour you like
- Hole punch, tape and a ruler

How to make

1. Fold the piece of paper or card in half.
2. Along the top of the folded paper, measure 2.5cm (1 inch) from the fold and make a mark.
3. Along the bottom of the folded paper, measure 2.5cm (1 inch) from the other side and make a mark.
4. Then, draw a line from one mark to the other.
5. Fold the paper along the line.
6. Turn the paper over and fold the other side down to match.

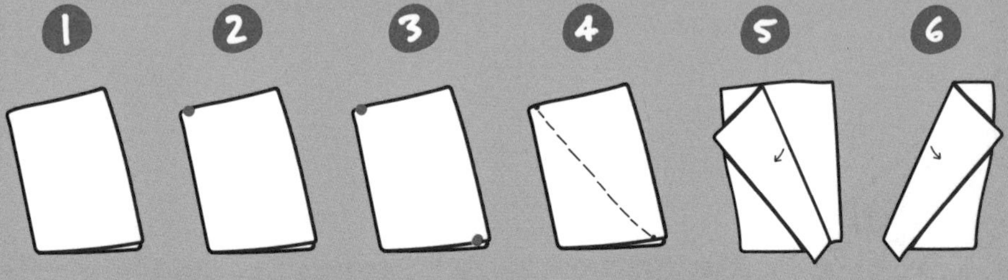

7. Then turn the paper back over so that it looks like it did in step 5. Tape along the middle line.
8. Put your skewer, bamboo stick or straw across the middle and tape it down. (If it is too long, ask a grown-up to help you cut it down to the right size.)
9. Turn your kite over and straighten out the middle flap.
10. Make a mark 5cm (2 inches) down from the top of the flap. Put tape over both sides of the mark to make it stronger, then punch a hole there.
11. Tie your string through this hole. Use a double knot.
12. Tape some ribbon to the bottom of your kite, then it is ready to fly!

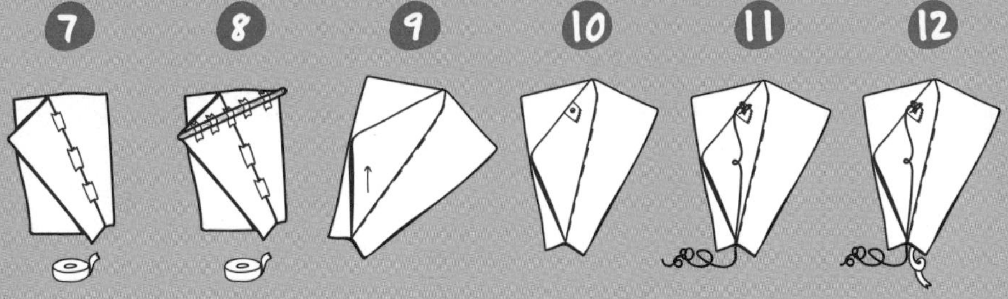

Tips

- Decorate your kite with pens, glitter, or whatever you like!
- Before flying the kite, make sure the middle flap is out straight.
- Try on a day where it is breezy but not too windy.
- If the kite starts to fall, pull the string tighter.
- If the kite looks like it is tugging on the string, unravel a bit more string to give it more freedom.
- Be patient, it takes a bit of practice to fly a kite!

Making my kite

Date: ______________________________

Where did you make your kite?

____

How difficult or easy was it to make?

____

What does your kite look like?

Draw it or stick in a photo.

Flying my kite

Date: ______________________________

Where did you go to fly your kite?

____

Who did you go with?

____

What was the weather like?

____

Did the kite fly well? What happened?

____

____

Rate this activity:

Trying yoga

Yoga isn't just about stretching, it's about focusing on your body and how it feels when you move and breathe.

Try out each of these yoga poses while breathing slowly and deeply. Think about what you can feel happening to your body.

1. Cat pose

On your hands and knees, start in a tabletop shape with a flat back. Then, as you breathe out, gently move your head down and bring your tummy up, making your back curved. Enjoy how it feels to stretch your back, then breathe out and lower back down into a tabletop shape.

2. Cow pose

Like the cat pose, start in a tabletop shape with a flat back. Then, as you breathe out, lift your head up to the sky and stick your bum in the air! Enjoy how it feels to stretch your back the other way, then breathe out and lower back down into a tabletop shape.

3. Child's pose

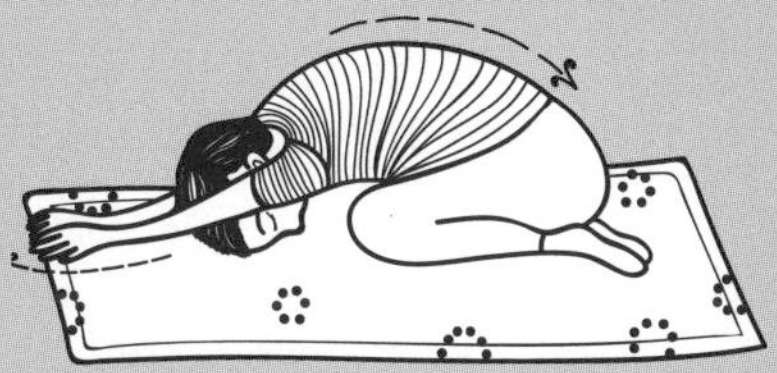

Start by kneeling on the floor with your feet together behind you. Sit back into your heels. Then, as you breathe out, bring your chest down onto your thighs and stretch your arms out in front of you, placing your hands on the floor. Relax and breathe for a minute before sitting back up.

4. Snake pose

Start by lying out flat with your belly on the ground. Put your hands flat on the floor next to your shoulders. Then, as you breathe out, push up onto your arms so your legs stay on the floor and your back curves. Look up at the ceiling and enjoy the stretch before lowering back down.

5. Tree pose

This is the pose that everyone thinks of when they hear 'yoga'. Stand up straight and put your hands together like you are praying. Then, as you breathe out, lift one leg and bend it to rest your foot on your other leg. See how long you can balance for, then lower your leg and try it with the other one.

Date: ____________________

Where did you try yoga?

____

How did your body feel when you were trying the yoga poses?

____

Which pose was your favourite?

____

Draw what you looked like doing yoga.

Invent a new yoga pose!
Draw what it looks like and don't forget to write down what you are going to call it.

Would you do yoga again? (Why or why not?)

Furry friends

If you don't have any pets, write and draw about your dream pet!

What pets do you have and what are their names?

Draw your pets here:

What are your pets' favourite kinds of food or treats?

What fun things do you do with your pet?

Do you think you are (or would be) good at looking after pets? Why or why not?

ПРИВЕТ!

Learning a new **language**

你好

What languages do you already know?

Your challenge is to find out how to write (or say) these 5 phrases in another language.

English phrases	Phrases in another language
'Hello my name is...'	
'I am 7 years old.'	
'How are you?'	
'I'm well, thank you!'	
'My favourite food is . . . .'	

(**Tip:** you could ask someone you know that speaks another language if they could help you, or you could use books or an online search to find out.)

Bonjour!

What language did you learn the 5 phrases in?

Why did you choose that language?

How did you find out the answers?
Did anyone help you?

How easy or difficult was it to say
the 5 phrases in another language?

If you could be really good at any other
language, which one would you choose and why?

Recipe: Spooky eyeball pasta

Has your meal ever stared back at you?! This spooky eyeball pasta is perfect for making at Halloween!

Ingredients

- Pasta of your choice
- Cherry tomatoes
- Mini mozzarella balls
- Olives or basil leaves
- Tomato passata
- Pesto

How to make

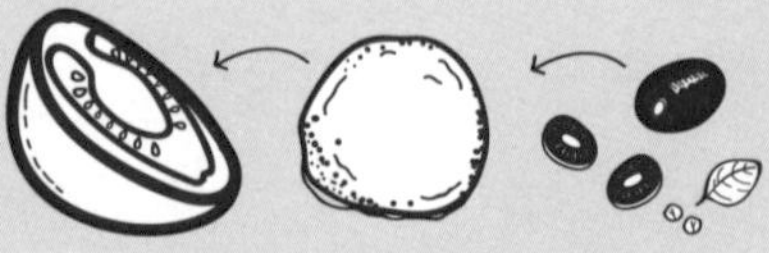

1. Cut each cherry tomato in half and each mozzarella ball in half.
2. Use a spoon to take the seeds out of the halved tomatoes, then stuff a halved mozzarella ball inside. (Put the eyeballs into the sockets!)
3. Cut small circles out of the basil leaves, or cut small circular slices of olive.
4. Put one circle onto the centre of each mozzarella ball to finish off your spooky eyeballs!
5. In one pan, boil the pasta. In another pan, heat up the passata and mix in the pesto.
6. Serve by placing the pasta into a bowl, then spooning on some of the sauce, then topping it off with a few spooky eyeballs!

REMEMBER! Safety is important, so don't try this on your own!

What did you enjoy most about making this recipe?

How did it taste?

Rate this recipe out of 5

1=Yuck!
5=Yum!

Draw or stick in a photo of what your spooky eyeball pasta looked like:

Wacky **races**

Invite your friends or family to take part in this tournament. **On your marks, get set, go!**

1. Crab race

For this wacky race, you'll need to run from your start line to the finish line in the style of a crab! Put both hands and both feet on the ground with your belly in the air: it's harder than it looks!

2. Backwards race

This race is exactly what it sounds like: racing backwards! (Just remember to keep looking behind you to see where you are going!)

3. Balancing race

Run while balancing something without dropping it. You could balance an egg on a spoon or a book on your shoulder.

4. Costume race

Have you ever seen a dinosaur race a fairy and a superhero? For this race, dress-up in your funniest costume (the sillier the better!).

5. Grasshopper race

For this wacky race, there is no finishing line. All start in the same place and make 10 big jumps. Whoever has leaped the furthest is the winner.

Where did you play wacky races, and who with?

For each type of race, give it a fun rating and write down who was the best at it.

Wacky race	**Fun rating**	**Who was best?**
Crab race	☆☆☆☆☆	
Backwards race	☆☆☆☆☆	
Balancing race	☆☆☆☆☆	
Costume race	☆☆☆☆☆	
Grasshopper race	☆☆☆☆☆	

What was your favourite thing about playing wacky races?

Pavement **chalks**

Have you ever used pavement chalks? You can draw all over the pavement and it's ok if you make a mess because it will easily wash away with a hose or when the rain comes!

Grab some pavement chalks and ask a grown-up to help you find a safe place to draw with them.

Need ideas?

Here are some fun things you can do with pavement chalks:

- Draw a picture
- Draw a hopscotch and jump in it
- Draw an obstacle course with different coloured lines to walk along, run along, or jump over
- Draw and play giant noughts and crosses
- Draw a maze
- Trace your shadow
- Draw a map (it could be a map of your imaginary house or den)

Date: ______________________

Where did you use your pavement chalks?

____

What did you draw with the chalks?

Write, draw, or stick in photos.

What was your favourite thing about drawing with your pavement chalks?

____

Rate this activity:

Creating a new **character**

Invent a new character that you would love to go on an adventure with!

What is your character's name?

What do they look like? What do they wear?

Draw them!

Where do they live?

Write or draw your answer.

What is their special talent or superpower?

What would you do on your adventures together?

Family are **friends** too!

Choose a member of your family who you think is also a good friend.

(It could be a brother, sister, cousin, aunt, uncle, grandparent, or someone else.)

What is their name? ______________________

How are they related to you? ______________

What do they look like?

Draw them or stick in a photo.

What is awesome about them?

What is your favourite thing to do together?

Write, draw, or stick in a photo.

Ask this family member to write a message to you here:

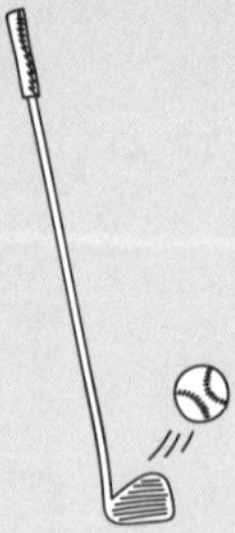

Inventing a new sport

Have you ever heard of frisbee golf? Chess boxing? Football tennis? Quidditch?

Invent your own sport. You could combine two sports or make up something new!

What would your new sport be called?

- -

What would be the aim of the sport?

(How would people win?)

- -

Write down 3 rules for your new sport:

1. ....
2. ....
3. ....

What would people need to play your new sport?

(Draw what the equipment would look like.)

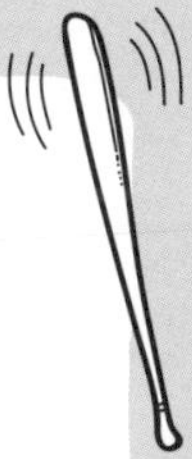

Where would people play your new sport?

(Draw what the arena, stadium, or pitch would look like.)

Do you think you would be good at it?

What makes me **laugh**

How often do you laugh?

Only sometimes ☐

Every day ☐

All the time! ☐

Write down something that makes you laugh.

(It could be a book, film, TV programme, or on the computer.)

____

What is the funniest joke you have EVER heard?

____

____

____

____

Who is the funniest person you know?

How do they make you laugh?

Do you think you are a funny person?

Why or why not?

Describe how it feels to make someone else laugh.

Quizzing my friends

Make up a quiz with 5 questions about you, then ask the quiz questions to 2 different friends to see how well they know you!

Question	Right answer
1.	
2.	
3.	
4.	
5.	

Here are some ideas for questions you could ask:

- What's my favourite/least favourite [something]?
- What's my middle name? When's my birthday?
- Do I prefer [this] or [that]? (e.g. pizza or chocolate?)

Date:

Name of first friend:

Question	Their answer	✓ or ✗ ?
1.		
2.		
3.		
4.		
5.		

Name of second friend:

Question	Their answer	✓ or ✗ ?
1.		
2.		
3.		
4.		
5.		

Who won? (Who knows you better?)

Welcome to the **talent** show!

Get your friends or family involved!

To host your own talent show, all you need is:

- A place to perform
- Some contestants with special talents
- Some people to be in your audience and watch the talent show
- Some people to be judges
- Paper and pens (to make scorecards)
- A prize for the winner!

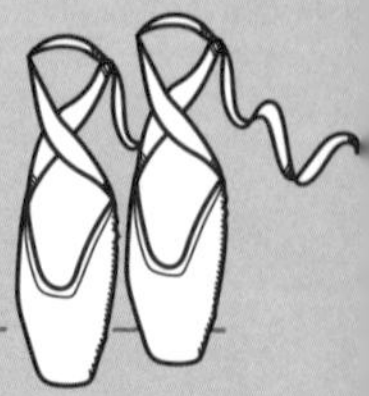

Date: ________________________________

Where will your talent show be?

____

Who will be the judge? (or judges?)

____

____

Write down who will enter your talent show, what their special talent will be, and what score they get after their performance.

Name	Talent	Score

What was your favourite part of the talent show?

Write, draw, or stick in a photo.

Designing my **dream home**

Design the home of your dreams!

What kind of home would it be?

(Mansion / treehouse / caravan / apartment / igloo / castle / cave / something else?)

What would the entrance be?

(A giant door / a tiny door / a secret tunnel / a zip line / a magic mirror / a trap door / something else?)

Where would it be?

(In the mountains / underwater / next door to where you live now / in the desert / in a city / in the sky / on another planet / somewhere else?)

What would be your favourite part of the home?

(Bedroom / kitchen / bathroom / games room / cinema / swimming pool / garden / sweets room / home library / stable / zoo / something else?)

What would your home look like?

Draw it here (the outside or the inside!).

Visiting a **planetarium**

A planetarium is a building with a domed roof where you can see stars, planets and constellations projected inside. Ask a grown-up to help you plan a visit to a planetarium and record your experience here:

Date:

If you can't visit a planetarium, go outside to look at the night sky on a clear night.

Which planetarium did you visit?

Who did you go with?

Describe your trip in 3 words:

Write down any interesting facts you learned during your visit to the planetarium:

Draw something interesting that you saw:

My favourite **outfit**

What is your favourite outfit?

Draw it or stick in a photo.

Why is it your favourite?

(Do you like the colours? The pattern? How it feels?)

Being a 7-year-old **fashion** designer

Design an awesome outfit that you would wear to an amazing party. You can draw or stick bits of material to the page.

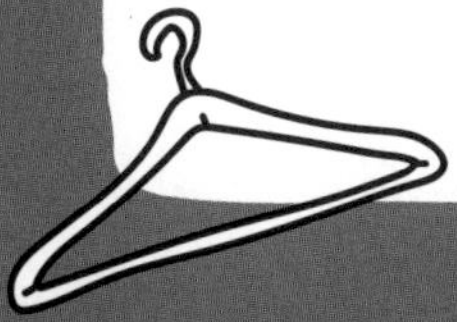

My awesome year being 7

You can write, draw, or stick things in!

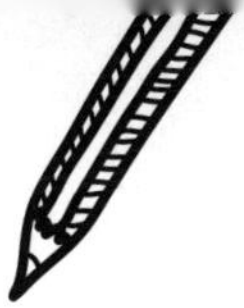

A note to grown-ups

You can join in the fun too by sharing experiences together, discussing the activities and celebrating accomplishments throughout the year! And remember to help with some of the recipes and other tricky tasks.

Follow us on Instagram @Collins4Parents where we'll be hosting regular competitions and giveaways as well as giving you extra ideas to make the year **even more awesome!** Share your experiences with the book using the hashtag #MyAwesomeYearBeing

My Awesome Year series

9780008372606

9780008372613

9780008372620

9780008372637

9780008372644

My year of **fun**

January	**February**
March	**April**
May	**June**